1-7-11

Jason –

May your journey
lead you to great
things and much happiness!

Mrs. C.

AROUND
THE
CAMPFIRE

AROUND THE CAMPFIRE

DEVOTIONALS FOR THE SPORTSMAN

The quoted ideas expressed in this book (but not scripture verses) are not, in all cases, exact quotations, as some have been edited for clarity and brevity. In all cases, the author has attempted to maintain the speaker's original intent. In some cases, quoted material for this book was obtained from secondary sources, primarily print media. While every effort was made to ensure the accuracy of these sources, the accuracy cannot be guaranteed.

For additions, deletions, corrections, or clarifications in future editions of this text, please contact Paul Shepherd, Executive Director for Elm Hill Books.
Email pshepherd@elmhillbooks.com.

Scripture quotations are taken from:

The Holy Bible, New International Version (NIV) Copyright © 1973, 1978, 1984, by International Bible Society. Used by permission of Zondervan Publishing House. All rights reserved.

New Century Version (NCV) © 1987, 1988, 1991 by Word Publishing, a division of Thomas Nelson, Inc. All rights reserved. Used by permission.

The Holy Bible, New King James Version (NKJV) Copyright © 1982 by Thomas Nelson, Inc. Used by permission.

Cover Design by Karen Phillips
Page Layout by Bart Dawson

ISBN 1-4041-8443-0

Printed in the United States of America

DEDICATED TO:

MY LORD AND SAVIOR, JESUS CHRIST,
MY LOVING WIFE ANGIE
AND SONS TUCKER AND TANNER,
AND MY DAD FOR TAKING ME FISHING.

TABLE OF CONTENTS

INTRODUCTION   11

OUT OF AFRICA   13
DEER MISSES   17
GETTING CLOSE   21
TOO BUSY TO HUNT   24
CURIOSITY KILLED THE SNAKE   27
WOODS & WATER WORSHIP   30
ZEBRA STRIPES   33
TURN YOUR RADIO ON   37
HUNTIN' BUDDIES!   40
A RIVER RUNS THROUGH IT   43
HOG WILD!   46
STRENGTH IN NUMBERS   49
BELOW THE SURFACE   52
WHERE'S THE TRUCK?   55
SEA SICK IN SOUTH MYRTLE   58
LIONS, TIGERS, AND BEARS   62
PEACE ON MCALPINE CREEK   65
TIME FOR TURKEY   69
THE ANCHOR HOLDS   73

THANKSGIVING TURKEY, VENISON & TRADITION	76
TIME TO REMEMBER	80
TALK TO THE ANIMALS	83
DEERSTAND DEVOTIONS	86
SAFARI JOURNAL	89
THE TROPHY KUDU	95
WARTHOG IN CAMP	98
LIVING IN A SHELL	102
SOAR LIKE AN EAGLE	105
LOST AT SEA	108
MAN'S BEST FRIEND	111
NO PLACE LIKE HOME	114
IN HIS SIGHTS	117
THE ONE THAT GOT AWAY	120
MAJOR IN MEN, MINOR IN FISH	123
THE GREAT KENTUCKY FLOOD	126
TRAIL OF TEARS	129
ROLES & RESPONSIBILITIES	133
A HUNTER'S RECIPE	137

INTRODUCTION

As the deer pants for streams of water,
so my soul pants for you, O God.
Psalm 42:1 NIV

For the last few years, the Lord has inspired me to write down what I have learned about Him through my experiences as an outdoorsman.

I quickly learned that my passion and zeal for hunting and fishing was greater than it was for God. It is a hard pill to swallow, but one we all need to take. How many of us get more excited for the coming deer season than for church on Sunday? Believe me, I have many times.

Around the Campfire is a devotional for just about anybody, not just outdoorsmen. We are drawn to a campfire for its warmth and glow, or to roast a hot dog or marshmallow. All is right with the world as we listen to stories told of days gone by. We marvel at God's Creation from the mountains to the seas. The beauty and purity of wildlife and nature captivate us. You don't have to be a sportsman to appreciate what God has created.

It is my hope and prayer for those who read this book, that your life may be touched in a new and special way. Stop, look, and listen to what God may teach you through all He has created and with which He has blessed us. So pull up a log around the campfire, take a load off, and enjoy the warmth and fellowship with me.

OUT OF AFRICA

Happiness makes a person smile,
but sadness can break a person's spirit.
Proverbs 15:13 NCV

The trip of a lifetime began for me and my hunting buddies with an 18-hour plane ride halfway around the world to the Dark Continent—Africa.

Our base camp was located on the Umsuluzi River in the KwaZulu-Natal province of South Africa. The history of the region is quite interesting. Just miles from our camp, Zulu warriors and British forces had engaged in a fierce battle. And now, here we were, hunting with Zulu Afrika Safaris in the land of Shaka Zulu.

Despite the newborn peace in South Africa, you could sense the hostility and animosity of racial and cultural differences. Along with our guide or "professional hunter," we were always accompanied in the bush by two Zulu trackers as we searched for Blue Wildebeest, Impala, Kudu and Warthog. The predators in the area included the Jackal and Leopard. The sensation I had standing alone in the bush was much different than in the hardwoods of North Carolina. I never worry too much about a raccoon or bobcat pouncing on me during deer season. In Africa, you play the role of both the hunter and the hunted. The unpredictability of nature is part of the thrill of the hunt.

But this trip to Africa was more than a hunt: it was a life-changing experience. The animals we harvested were a mere bonus. The Discovery Channel and National Geographic don't do the country justice. The raw, undeveloped beauty of the landscape is awesome. It is a look at God's Creation, untouched and unspoiled by man. The animals you picture on Noah's Ark roam freely on the plains. A giraffe standing 18 feet tall, looked over the top of a tree at me from only 30 yards away! At any moment I expected someone to say, "Welcome to Jurassic Park!"

As astonishing as the animals and environment are, the people and their culture moved and captivated me. The two Zulu trackers with us throughout our expedition were "human spotting scopes." I thought my eyes were good for spotting game! With the naked eye, they could spot an Impala in the bush at 400 yards and tell you if it was a trophy or not. I tried to get to know them through our Professional

Hunter, but they could speak only a few words of English. I did learn one tracker had three wives and fifteen children. How I desperately I wanted to speak to them in their native tongue, to know them better and learn more of their way of life.

The primitive existence of the Zulu people takes you back to a different age. Subsistence living is a foreign concept to most Americans. It humbled me. I was no different in God's eyes than the Zulus, merely born in a different place. We are all beautifully and wonderfully made by God. There are a few things cultural differences could not divide between us. While there is a language barrier, it felt good to see them smile when I would great them with a smile. A smile has the capability of changing attitudes and calming fears without the spoken word.

Try smiling a little more. A smile may be the only Jesus some will ever see. God created the world, Africa, the animals, and man in 6 days. On the 7th day, He rested, and with a smile said, "It is good!"

THOUGHTS & REFLECTIONS

_____

_____

_____

_____

_____

_____

_____

_____

_____

_____

_____

_____

_____

_____

_____

_____

_____

_____

_____

_____

DEER MISSES

If we confess our sins, He is faithful and just to forgive us our sins and to cleanse us from all unrighteousness.

1 John 1:9 NKJV

How many of you have done all the right stuff in bow hunting, only to blow the shot when it counts? Boy, I sure have. It's happened to me several times. After you miss a shot, nausea inevitably starts to come over you. For just a brief moment, you're ready to sell all your hunting equipment on Ebay®.

I had already missed one deer early in the North Carolina bow season. With a few adjustments, I got back in the stand to try give it another go. In my mind, I reviewed the hunter's success checklist:

1. Good stand placement … check
2. Wind direction … check
3. Scent covered … check
4. Mossy Oak camo … check
5. Bow, arrows, release … triple check

All of the time, energy, and money I put into deer hunting came down to just a few brief seconds. A beautiful 6-point buck walked up the trail on which I was set up. The wind direction was perfect as he walked in "the zone." It was time! Browsing aimlessly at 10 yards away, I drew my bow and released the arrow. I made the best shot on a stump I'd ever seen! I don't think I could duplicate it if I tried. But the deer ran off with that big white tail up, wagging it back and forth as if to taunt me. Nausea set in.

The first time I drew back my bow, I realized that I could not see through my peep sight in low-light conditions. I could see the deer, but when you looked at the target through a small hole, everything was distorted. It was the second deer in two weeks I had missed because of the same problem. I thought I had done everything right to make the hunt a success but had failed to take action when I found something wrong.

This failure reminded me of my relationship with God. Sound familiar to you? How many times do we make a mistake in life and fail to learn from it? I miss the mark of obedience to God all the time without correcting the problem. We are often convicted of sin in our lives but choose to ignore it. Like any root problem, it doesn't go away until we confess it and turn from it.

I knew the peep sight on my bow would pose a problem at dawn and dusk. I chose not to deal with it. The hard lesson: Do not ignore problems with your bow—or your life. Those deer were happy though!

THOUGHTS & REFLECTIONS

_____

_____

_____

_____

_____

_____

_____

_____

_____

_____

_____

_____

_____

_____

_____

_____

_____

_____

_____

_____

_____

_____

_____

_____

_____

_____

_____

_____

_____

GETTING CLOSE

When you do things, do not let selfishness or pride be your guide. Instead, be humble and give more honor to others than to yourselves. Do not be interested only in your own life, but be interested in the lives of others.

Philippians 2:3, 4 NCV

Mossy Oak, a camouflage-design company, has a slogan for advertising I found interesting. It simply stated, "It's sometimes more than a critter you want to get close to!" The underlying meaning of the words: Spend time with your family and friends. It is easy for a hunter to become so captivated by the challenge and adventure. You forget what is truly meaningful in life.

The relationships with our children, family, and friends are far more important than the 10-point buck harvested last year. If we spent as much time and energy "getting close" to the people in our lives as we do stalking animals, the reward and harvest would be great and bountiful. In hunting terms, "We can't see the forest for the trees!" With so many things in life to keep us busy, it is simple to take for granted the people who really make the difference.

My most memorable hunts were not the countless times I went to the woods alone. Rather, it was walking the edge of a field with a friend looking for a covey of quail, talking on the two-way radios from tree stand to tree stand, telling stories on the front porch of the cabin or around the campfire, showing my son a deer track, or cutting the shirttail of a friend who just missed.

These are the experiences I will remember years from now. Many of us lost loved ones last year we dearly miss. It is my hope and prayer we would spend more time hunting for hearts and "getting close" to the people God has put in our lives.

THOUGHTS & REFLECTIONS

_____

_____

_____

_____

_____

_____

TOO BUSY TO HUNT

*Come to me, all of you who are tired and have heavy loads,
and I will give you rest.*
Matthew 11:28 NCV

Have you ever heard of someone being too busy to hunt? I sure have! In fact, I've said it a few times myself this past season. Life has a way of moving along and changing a few priorities. I've got a wonderful wife and two little boys. The discretionary time I once had to jump in a tree stand or fish early on a Saturday morning is now occupied by those young 'uns. They are worth every minute, too!

Despite not hunting as much as usual, the experience becomes more than predator and prey. Yes, the challenge is invigorating, but so is the experience and fellowship. The quantity of my trips has decreased, but the quality has definitely increased. I appreciate more the precious time that is spent outdoors, whether it's with friends, or just one-on-one with God. I find it amazing that no matter how old I get, or how busy I am, the woods and water are timeless entities. They never change. In an instant, I can be taken back to my childhood, free of responsibility, full of innocence, and searching for adventure. We all miss the "carefree" days, but they are not far away when you rest in God's Creation, the great outdoors.

I believe the timelessness of the outdoors is not by chance. God created everything that way. God is timeless: He was, He is, and He always will be! God sent His Son, Jesus Christ to die for you and me, before we were ever born. This is the kind of love and power that formed all of Creation in just 6 days. It is no wonder why He rested on the seventh day! If God in all His power can see fit to take a rest, then by granny, so can we. Let's go back to Sunday being a day of rest, relaxation, and reflection.

If you are at a stage in your life where you find you are too busy, don't miss the forest for the trees. Take a step back, appreciate all God has blessed you with— your wife, children, grandchildren, parents, friends, home, health, and so on. Take time to thank the Lord for Who He is and what He has done. He has created all you see outdoors that we may know He is God. Get back to your first love. Too busy? Enter into God's rest by spending time in His Creation.

THOUGHTS & REFLECTIONS

_____

_____

_____

_____

_____

_____

_____

_____

_____

_____

_____

_____

_____

_____

CURIOSITY KILLED THE SNAKE

Let no one say when he is tempted, "I am tempted by God";
for God cannot be tempted by evil, nor does He Himself
tempt anyone. But each one is tempted when he is drawn away
by his own desires and enticed.
James 1:13, 14 NKJV

At my hunting lodge in South Carolina, we guide hunters to deer, turkey and wild boar. It is not uncommon to see venomous snakes like rattlesnakes, cottonmouths, and copperheads. They don't scare me as long as I can see them before they see me. However, I do wear snake-proof boots as a precaution.

Late one evening in early September, I drove into our swamp tract to pick up some boar hunters. As I drove past the gate to the property, I noticed a rattlesnake, 4 to 5 feet in length, stretched across the road. It was as big around as my arm. Now I happen to like snakes, but I wasn't going to try some of that "Croc Hunter" stuff like Steve Irwin! Animal rights activists, don't be alarmed. I didn't kill the snake. Keep reading.

As I drove over to the big rattler, he didn't move

a bit. I stopped the truck with the left front tire barely sitting on the snake. With the snake rattling aggressively, I cautiously looked out the window to find him biting the fire out of a perfectly good Michelin. Boy, was he mad! He was squirting venom all over that tire!

Now don't worry, the snake was fine. He slithered off into the brush just a little aggravated. I immediately exited the vehicle to use what I learned watching that "CSI" TV show. It was time to investigate the scene of the "bite and run" accident! Upon close investigation, here's what I found: multiple puncture wounds to the tire exterior, large amounts of venom dripping from the tire, and one broken-off fang from the culprit. Case closed! If I'm lying…I'm dying! That snake broke one fang right off in the tire and I pulled it out. It has become a standing joke at the lodge to warn hunters of our "snaggletooth rattlesnake."

You know the 'ol saying, "Curiosity killed the cat?" Well, it almost killed a snake that day. The story does show us how dangerous it can be to threaten a creature in its natural habitat. If we get too close, we are liable to get bit. Our temptations in life can lead to the same result. When we are tempted and fall into sin, it rears its ugly head and angrily bites us.

Don't let curiosity or temptation bring you down. Be strong in the Lord, keep the faith—and keep your distance.

THOUGHTS & REFLECTIONS

_____

_____

_____

_____

_____

_____

_____

_____

_____

_____

_____

WOODS & WATER WORSHIP

Be still and know that I am God;
I will be exalted among the nations, I will be exalted in the earth!
Psalm 46:10 NKJV

It was a cool, crisp February morning in the low country swamps of South Carolina. I struggled to stay warm as I sat in a tree stand in the dark, anxiously awaiting the break of day. The animal I hunted was the Russian Wild Boar.

Minutes passed like hours as the sun procrastinated its appearance on the horizon. The woods were silent at the moment. The temperature is always its coldest right before daybreak. I began to ask myself, "Why am I here?" as I shivered and shook. The answer to my question came quickly as sunlight filtered through the Spanish moss hanging from the branches of the majestic water oak.

As always, it was as if God turned on a light switch as a new day dawned. I remembered what the preacher had said about worship. "Worship is simply humbling yourself before God, realizing that we are not worthy, but He is!" My experience in the woods then became more than just a hunt.

The call to worship started with the warm sunrise and the caw of a crow. The choir, made up of squirrels, songbirds, and woodpeckers, prepared my heart for the message. Like a son sitting on his father's lap, I looked through the forest canopy to my Heavenly Father. What do you say? Whatever is on your heart...the good, the bad, and the ugly! I began to understand that worship is not a place or a program; rather, it is seeking God and recognizing Him for who He is and what He has done for us!

The woods and water worship service drew to a close as nine wild boars came grunting by my tree stand, like ushers passing by the pew. I didn't shoot, but enjoyed the moment for what it was. Once again, I was grateful to God for another life lesson through the wonders of His Creation, the Great Outdoors.

Thoughts & Reflections

_____

_____

_____

_____

ZEBRA STRIPES

Two sparrows cost only a penny, but not even one of them can die without your Father's knowing it. God even knows how many hairs are on your head. So don't be afraid. You are worth much more than many sparrows.
Matthew 10:29-31 NCV

As we were maneuvering through the thorn bush, the Zebra stallion alerted the herd of present danger. He was the leader, the alpha male. At that point, I realized that we were in his domain, the African bush! This is no zoo. There were no fences or boundaries. The entire herd looked to him for warning signs of any predators nearby. With our professional hunter (Tobie) leading the way, I mimicked his every move. We couldn't seem to get close enough. The stallion continually slipped through the thicket, just out of range.

Like a Leopard, we crawled on our hands and knees to flank the herd. My heart was pounding as the thrill of the hunt became more real. Tobie predicted the direction in which the Zebra would move, so we slid into position, looking through a small gap in the dense cover. I grew anxious like a cat, ready to pounce at the right time. Several mares moved through the thicket as the big stallion brought up the rear. As he moved briskly through the opening, the shot was taken and the stalk was over.

My buddy Chip shot a nice Zebra that afternoon. As we admired the markings and stripes of his Zebra, Tobie began to point out the distinct features of the hide. He contrasted the stripes of Chip's Zebra to the stripes of mine. The differences were subtle but quite unique. My Zebra had some big spots between the stripes on either side of the spine. Chip's Zebra had a stripe on the face that formed a teardrop. A stripe down the side might fork at the bottom. From a distance, all the Zebra looked the same to me. Intrigued by Tobie's observations, I asked, "Why are the markings and stripes so different?" He said, "Each Zebra has unique markings that distinguish it from all other Zebra…it gives them character."

Tobie went on to say that a baby Zebra identifies its mother by her stripes! With several females in the herd, the baby imprints the mother within days after birth by identifying her special pattern of stripes. Unlike most animals that rely upon smell to identify parents or offspring, the baby Zebra identifies it's mother's beautiful and unique stripes.

Did you know that God created each of us to be special? There is no one person like you in the world. God knows our physical, mental and emotional characteristics. He gave us unique qualities and abilities. Note Jesus' words in the verses from Matthew 10:29-31. Now I know that some of us don't have many hairs to count. But we all did at one time. Like the Zebra, God created each of us to be unique and special. Thank you God, for loving me just as I am.

THOUGHTS & REFLECTIONS

_____

_____

_____

_____

_____

_____

_____

TURN YOUR RADIO ON

The effective, fervent prayer of a righteous man avails much.
James 5:16b NKJV

It is amazing to see how far hunting technology has come in just the last decade. There are more gadgets out there than Carter's got little liver pills. From GPS to two-way radios, you can find about anything you need. On a recent wild boar hunt in the low country of South Carolina, I had the rare opportunity to use hand-held radios. My buddy Chip handed me one as we departed for the evening hunt. I had only used these radios a few times before.

Settled in my tree stand, I turned on my radio, making sure it was on the same channel Chip was. I called for him numerous times throughout the evening to fight some of the boredom and mosquitoes. But there was no response, only silence! I began to worry about him a little. When we met up later, I asked him, "Why didn't you talk on the radio?" He quickly replied, "I didn't have it turned on!" Two-way radios aren't much good if one is not turned on.

You know, our line of communication to God is "two-way" through prayer. We call upon God whenever we need Him and He always hears our call. His radio doesn't have an off switch because it's always on! The problem exists when God speaks to us and we don't have our "radio" on. Chip couldn't hear me because he wasn't prepared to receive my call.

God often speaks to us in a still small voice. We need to prepare our hearts and minds to hear His call. Turn your "radio" on, God always does.

THOUGHTS & REFLECTIONS

_____

_____

_____

_____

_____

_____

_____

HUNTIN' BUDDIES!

Jesus answered, "'Love the Lord your God with all your heart, all your soul, and all your mind.' This is the first and most important command. And the second command is like the first: 'Love your neighbor as you love yourself.'"
Matthew 22:37-39 NCV

It's summertime and deer season is just around the corner. The "fever" or "itch" starts to come over a hunter about July. It's time to hit the woods and do a little pre-season scouting. I recently attempted to slip out of the house to check out a new place to hunt. Slipping out is easier said then done. My wife used to be the only one to gain permission from before leaving the premises. Now with two young boys, they have joined the approval committee.

I threw on a pair of camo brush pants, an old t-shirt and headed for the door. "Where are you going Daddy?"

My oldest had made me out! "Uh, uh, I'm just running an errand," I replied.

"Why are you wearing camo Daddy?" he said. At this point, I feel like the Grinch caught stealing Christmas stuff by Cindy Lou "who was no more than two." You remember the scene I'm talking about.

Now that you know how I felt at that moment, my boy sadly said, "You're going to the hunt club. Can I go? We're huntin' buddies." I was unable to respond for what seemed like hours. In what was only a few seconds, my young boy reminded me once again what life is really about. Children live to experience life with parents. That boy loves to put on his camo overalls and cap and ride in the truck to look for deer. Not ever old enough to hunt, he relates to me through our time spent in the outdoors. We can never spend too much time fishing, hunting, or hiking with our children and grandchildren.

While a little boy taught me a life lesson, God took the opportunity to show me the spiritual significance of the event. How often do we cover ourselves and selfishly slip through life without spending time with God? Good camo won't even hide us from God. Adam and Eve tried the "fig-leaf" camo pattern and it didn't work too well in the Garden of Eden. As we head out the door, God seems to surprise us with the love and innocence of a child who says, "Where are you going? We're buddies. I miss you and only want to spend time with you!" Whether it is God or family calling you, spend time with your "buddies."

THOUGHTS & REFLECTIONS

_____

_____

_____

_____

_____

_____

_____

_____

_____

_____

_____

_____

_____

_____

_____

_____

_____

"A RIVER RUNS THROUGH IT"

Trust in the Lord with all your heart, and lean not on your own understanding; In all your ways acknowledge Him, and He shall direct your paths.
Proverbs 3:5, 6 NKJV

In the blockbuster movie, *A River Runs Through It*, Robert Redford's character grew up with a passion for fly-fishing for trout. What awesome scenery in that flick! There's nothing like slipping on the waders, putting on the felt-bottom boots, and wading a pristine trout stream.

I attended Mars Hill College in the Appalachian Mountains of western North Carolina. The area lays claim to some of the best trout water in the country. One of my personal favorites is the Nantahala River near the NC/TN line. Many locals will argue that the surrounding countryside truly is "God's Country."

I'll never forget a foggy morning when I stepped in the river and a bobcat was watching me from the bank on the other side. I thanked the Lord instantly for such an awesome sight. The bobcat disappeared in the laurel bushes. And I soon caught a nice rainbow.

I proceeded to work downstream from hole to

hole. Now some folks prefer to fish upstream, but it is usually easier to go with the flow than to fight the current in big water like the Nantahala.

In the same way, we tend to fight the swift current in our lives. We live the way we want, do what we want, when we want. The happiness we experience doing it "our way" is only temporary when compared to the joy found in doing God's will. God has a perfect plan for our lives. It is up to us to yield to His direction for our lives. I am reminded of the classic hymn, "Trust and obey, for there's no other way..." It's a whole lot easier to fish downstream. Try it sometime.

THOUGHTS & REFLECTIONS

_____

_____

_____

_____

_____

_____

_____

_____

_____

_____

_____

_____

_____

_____

_____

_____

_____

_____

_____

_____

_____

_____

_____

_____

_____

_____

HOG WILD!

As for me, I will call upon God, and the Lord shall save me.
Evening and morning and at noon I will pray,
and cry aloud, And He shall hear my voice.
Psalm 55:16, 17 NKJV

Have you ever been so afraid that you literally asked God to deliver you? It sounds funny, but I've done so on many occasions.

During my freshman year in college, I hunted and fished more than I ever studied. One of my favorite hunting spots was Flattop Mountain in Yancey County. You talk about beautiful country! Back in those days, I often hunted the mountains by myself. Not the wisest thing to do.

I was bow-hunting miles from nowhere late one evening. As I slipped along a logging road, I could hear something rustling the leaves in the hollow above me. It sounded like several deer scratching the forest floor in search of acorns. The stalk was on. I went into "stealth" mode! The sounds led me into a laurel thicket. On all fours, I inched closer to the persistent sounds. Suddenly, right before my eyes, was a bunch of black-haired Russian Boar. My heart panicked as I searched for a nearby tree to climb. But there was not tree around that would hold my 240 lb. self. I was "as nervous as a cat on a rotten limb." I actually closed my eyes and prayed, "Lord, please help me! I'll never eat bacon or barbecue again!" Boy, have I broken that promise since then.

We can really pray when we are in trouble, can't we? It is so easy not to call upon God when times are good and all is right with the world. Well, that day the Lord heard my plea, as I was able to slowly crawl away undetected. I learned my lesson: Call upon the Lord in all things, before they've gone "hog wild."

Thoughts & Reflections

_____

_____

_____

_____

_____

_____

STRENGTH IN NUMBERS

And let us consider one another in order to stir up love and good works, not forsaking the assembling of ourselves together, as is the manner of some, but exhorting one another...
Hebrews 10:24, 25 NKJV

Very few animals that inhabit the earth are loners. I'm sure you could probably come up with a few. But many species are group or family oriented. You often see a herd of deer, a flock of turkeys, or a covey of quail. There were many hunting trips where I just wanted to see one deer, let alone a herd!

Take time to study the behavior of any animal. They are very relational with their own kind. Mothers tend to their offspring. Young animals joyfully play together. I love to watch squirrels chase each other up and down an oak tree, or see fawns running in circles in an open field. When it comes to survival, animals find solace and strength in numbers. A covey of quail will huddle close together when a predator is nearby. If you mess with one hornet, you mess with the whole hive!

God created us in the same way. We, too, are creatures that need family and fellowship. It is not meant for us to go it alone in life. For that reason, it is very important for us to be a part of a church fellowship. Regardless of the denomination, be close to the Body of Christ. Read John 15. A branch apart from the vine cannot bear fruit. That is a fundamental principal in Gardening 101 and in life. Open your heart to others and be accountable. It is then that you will find strength in numbers.

THOUGHTS & REFLECTIONS

_____

_____

_____

_____

_____

_____

_____

_____

_____

_____

_____

_____

_____

_____

_____

_____

_____

_____

_____

_____

_____

BELOW THE SURFACE

The LORD does not look at the things man looks at.
Man looks at the outward appearance,
but the LORD looks at the heart.
1 Samuel 16:7 NIV

My wife and I went on a cruise for our honeymoon to several islands in the Caribbean. On Barbados, we had the opportunity to do some snorkeling. For the avid outdoorsman, anything to do with animals or fish is worthwhile.

Have you noticed that when you look at the surface of the ocean, all you see is waves, foam, and a little seaweed? It is when we peer below the surface that we gain a completely new perspective. Magnificently colored fish swim peacefully in and around the jagged coral reef. It's as if you were actually inside a well-decorated fish bowl! There is more variety in sea creatures than people at an airport. You would never know how spectacular the ocean is by merely looking at the surface. God didn't play around when He created the ocean! I wonder sometimes what He thought of the movie, *Jaws*. It sure made me think twice about body surfing.

How often do we form our opinion about things based upon what we see? All the time. It is our nature. It can be especially dangerous in our relationships with others. We cast judgment upon people with little knowledge of who they really are. Aren't you glad God didn't take a long look at you and say, "By the looks of this one, he's not worth a plug nickel." Rather, God looks beyond our appearance to our heart, the very core of our existence, and sees us for who we are.

Try a little "spiritual" snorkeling, get below the surface, and find what is genuine and real in life—and in others.

THOUGHTS & REFLECTIONS

_____

_____

_____

_____

_____

_____

_____

_____

_____

_____

_____

_____

_____

_____

_____

_____

_____

_____

_____

_____

_____

_____

_____

_____

_____

_____

_____

WHERE'S THE TRUCK?

Trust in the Lord, and do good; Dwell in the land, and feed on His faithfulness. Delight yourself also in the Lord...
Commit your way to the Lord, trust also in Him...
Rest in the Lord, and wait patiently for Him...
Psalm 37:3-7 NKJV

Have you ever been lost in the woods? Man, I've been lost in the dark and the light! It's not difficult to lose your bearings without a compass, landmarks, and reflective tape. I forgot—we've got GPS now.

Most of my early hunting experiences took place in the rugged mountains of North Carolina. You hike a few miles in, cross over a few ridges and hollows, and wish you had a flare gun. I had been tracking some fresh deer tracks that led me astray. No sidewalks or street signs. No gas stations or payphones to ask for directions. I'm normally good at marking where I have been, but my mind was focused entirely on the hunt. I soon realized it was approaching nightfall and I needed to find the truck. I kept telling myself, the truck should be directly over the next ridge. No chance! Being completely lost is a frightening experience. It is the same feeling you get when you become separated from your folks in a huge department store—lost! We've all been there one time or another.

In the same way, we are lost in this world without God. We try to find our way through life with everything else but God. With no direction, we wander aimlessly from person to person and place to place. We can find real comfort in Proverbs 3:5, 6 (NKJV) *Trust in the Lord with all your heart, and lean not on your own understanding; in all your ways acknowledge Him, and He shall direct your paths.* Look it up again whenever you ask yourself, "Where's the truck?"

THOUGHTS & REFLECTIONS

_____

_____

_____

_____

_____

_____

SEA SICK IN SOUTH MYRTLE

The way of a fool is right in his own eyes,
but he who heeds counsel is wise.
Proverbs 12:15 NKJV

Seasickness. Have you ever been there, done that? Unfortunately, I must raise my hand. I have suffered knee injuries that paled in comparison to being seasick. It was my first deep-sea fishing trip. A friend and his father had booked an all day trip on a "party" boat out of South Myrtle Beach, South Carolina. I would soon find out the trip was no party.

Our destination was the Gulf Stream to fish for grouper and red snapper. Having never been out on the open sea in a boat, my friend recommended I take some of those pills to keep you from getting sick. I pridefully said, "No thank you, I'll be fine." Famous last words of a fool. Why do we men have such big egos? The boat was no more than a mile from the marina, and I was giving it the 'ol heave ho. To make matters worse, the ocean was rough and waves were crashing over the bow of the boat. Everyone was below the deck except myself and another prideful guy with the same problem. I prayed that the Lord would calm the sea just as He did on Galilee. I finally understood how Gregory Peck must have felt strapped to the back of that white whale. I continued to pray, "Lord, get me to the nearest piece of dry land, do not pass go, do not collect $200." I never wet a line that day but did live to tell about it!

So often we depend on God to bail us out as we blame Him for circumstances we created. Remember that He blessed us with a keen mind and spirit to make good decisions. God is working behind the scenes without our knowing it. I am always reminded of the man who was caught in a great flood. As the floodwaters rose, he stood atop the chimney of his home. He prayed hard for God to deliver him from peril. A boat came by soon after and urged him to get in. The man said, "No thank you, God will deliver me." A second boat came by and his response was the same. With the water about to overtake him, a helicopter hovered above.

The rescue team lowered a ladder and with a megaphone shouted, "Sir, climb up the ladder, you don't have much time!"

Again the man responded, "My God will deliver me!" The man perished in the flood soon after. When he stood before God in Heaven he asked, "Lord, I had faith that you would deliver me from the great flood. Why didn't you?"

God answered, "I sent you two boats and a helicopter!"

Remember that God often works through the lives of people to accomplish His purposes. By the way, the next time I went deep-sea fishing...I took those pills.

THOUGHTS & REFLECTIONS

_____

_____

_____

_____

_____

_____

_____

_____

LIONS, TIGERS, AND BEARS

Be sober, be vigilant; because your adversary the devil walks about like a roaring lion, seeking whom he may devour.

1 Peter 5:8 NKJV

In the southeastern region of "God's Country," there is an abundance of wildlife, which includes deer, bear, turkey, and many other species. What you won't see much of are mountain lions, although they do inhabit the south. These cats are more commonly referred to as a cougar, panther, or puma. A lion in the south is more of a myth than a reality, as they are quite rare.

I hunted often with a friend at a hunt club in the low country of South Carolina. He had not hunted much before we met, and exploded with excitement in anticipation of each hunt. On one occasion, I gave him my old Winchester Model 94 30.30, and set him on the ground at the edge of a cut cornfield. When we met back at the cabin after the hunt, his face was as white as a sheet. He said he had seen a bobcat, and it scared him half to death. I laughed and explained to him that a bobcat is harmless. Interested in his encounter, I probed further and asked, "Did it have a pretty coat with black spots?" "No, it was solid, grayish-brown in color," he exclaimed. At this point, I thought that his inexperience in the field was the reason for the false identification. I then asked, "Did the cat have a bobbed tail?" He responded, "No, it had a body about 4 feet long, with a tail 2-3 feet long!" I knew in an instant that what he had seen was no bobcat or housecat. The mountain lion had come within 10 yards of him. Later, the state DNR confirmed there were some pumas in the area.

You know, the devil lurks about much like that mountain lion. My friend was unsure exactly what kind of animal it was. As Christians, it is important for us to know who the enemy is to keep from being attacked. Stay close to the Lord and His Word to discern whom the enemy is. Don't be caught off guard!

THOUGHTS & REFLECTIONS

_____

_____

_____

_____

_____

_____

_____

_____

_____

_____

_____

_____

_____

_____

_____

_____

_____

_____

_____

_____

_____

_____

_____

_____

PEACE ON McALPINE CREEK

Oh, that you had heeded My commandments!
Then your peace would have been like a river…
Isaiah 48:18 NKJV

Growing up in Charlotte, North Carolina was a wonderful experience. We lived in a development that in the 80s was on the border of town and country. Oh, how the South Charlotte area has changed! Our family would travel on Hwy. 51 from Pineville to Matthews, on an old two-lane road, with a 55-mph speed limit. You can't go 100 yards anymore without having to stop for something these days. No wonder I live in Union County now. I'll probably be living on the beach by the time the growth slows down!

Our property adjoined hundreds of acres of undeveloped woods and wetlands. McAlpine Creek was about 10 to 20 feet wide, and gracefully meandered behind our house. There was a well-beaten path through the hardwoods that led to the creek. That creek was home to many species of fish including bass, bream, catfish, and an occasional crappie.

When the Japanese beetles would invade Charlotte in the summer, I'd gather dozens at a time and put them into a cricket keeper. I'd grab my trusty Zebco 202 fishing rod, beetles, and my dog Rusty, and head out. Rusty, my faithful companion would watch anxiously from the bank, as I would catch fish by the tubful. Never was a beetle set free, unfortunately. If records were kept, I'll bet my eyeteeth that I've caught more fish out of McAlpine Creek than anyone in Mecklenburg County.

I never did keep one fish I caught from that creek. It was simply a safe haven for a young boy with a lot of energy. As I fished, I would whistle, "Bob white, bob white," and soon a quail would respond in kind. Thinking it was always the same bobwhite quail; I named him "Charlie." Charlie would always answer my call on McAlpine Creek.

With the increasing pressures of school and adolescence, I found refuge between its banks and peace in its waters. Find the McAlpine Creek in your life and talk to God there. Jesus says in Matthew 11:28, "Come to me, all you who are weary and burdened, and I will give you rest." I am reminded of those days on the creek when I hear the precious words in an old childhood song, "I've got peace like river, I've got peace like a river, I've got peace like a river in my soul."

THOUGHTS & REFLECTIONS

_____

_____

_____

_____

_____

_____

_____

_____

_____

_____

_____

_____

_____

_____

_____

_____

_____

_____

_____

THOUGHTS & REFLECTIONS

_____

_____

_____

_____

_____

_____

_____

_____

_____

_____

_____

_____

_____

_____

_____

_____

_____

_____

_____

_____

TIME FOR TURKEY

I have been crucified with Christ; it is no longer I who live,
but Christ lives in me; and the life which I now live
in the flesh I live by faith in the Son of God,
who loved me and gave Himself for me.
Galatians 2:20 NKJV

The alarm clock is blaring and dangerously close to getting blown up with a 12 gauge at four o'clock in the morning. Time to rise and shine for opening day of turkey season. For just a brief moment you lay there questioning your mental stability for getting up at this time of day. You know it's early when you say a morning prayer and jokingly think that the Lord isn't even up yet! Why do we torture ourselves purposefully? The answer is simple: For the love of the hunt. It is this thrill that drives us to extreme measures.

I'll never forget the year I woke up late on the opening day of Turkey Season in Madison County, North Carolina. I was so anxious to get to the woods before daylight that I put the "pedal to the metal." Unfortunately, a state trooper pulled me over doing 81 in a 55 mph zone. As the trooper approached the side of my truck, there I sat in full camo, owl hooter around my neck, and shotgun in the passenger's seat. He said, "Boy, where you goin' in such a hurry this mornin'?"

I quickly responded, "I'm sorry officer, but I was runnin' late for my turkey hunt!" I believe the trooper felt a little sorry for me that spring morning, but not enough to keep from giving me my first ticket at the age of 19.

I was still on a mission. To hear the bone-chilling gobble of a wild turkey amidst the tall hardwoods is an invigorating experience. The adrenaline rush is unbelievable! Suddenly, 4:00 AM doesn't seem all that early. I may have to join a support group like "Hunters Anonymous" for help. I can see it now, sitting in front of a bunch of guys in camo, as I emotionally mutter, "Hi, my name is Tom. And I am an obsessed hunter."

How much greater is our passion for God? He gave His very best to us in the person of His Son, Jesus Christ. Are we as fired up about going to church as we are to get to the woods? As hunters, we equip ourselves with the best gun, gadgets, and gear money can buy. We get up at "dark thirty" to hit the woods. Yet we struggle to get to church by 9:30 one morning a week.

Just as the challenge of the hunt requires our very best, God requires the same in our relationship with Him. May we seek Him with the same passion and zeal we show for the outdoors.

THOUGHTS & REFLECTIONS

_____

_____

_____

_____

_____

_____

_____

_____

_____

_____

_____

THE ANCHOR HOLDS

> *These two things cannot change: God cannot lie when He makes a promise, and he cannot lie when He makes an oath. These things encourage us who came to God for safety. They give us strength to hold on to the hope we have been given. We have this hope as an anchor for the soul, sure and strong...*
> Hebrews 6:18, 19 NCV

I believe I have been a fisherman since I was in the womb, or sometime soon after. My grandparents owned a trailer on a small lake outside Jackson, Michigan. It was their weekend getaway. It was also our family tradition to vacation there on the 4th of July. As a young boy, I lived for the day I could take out the 'ol rowboat by myself to fish. One of the best known "honey holes" was on the other side of the lake, and could only be fished by boat.

The day finally came when I was 8 years old. My Granddad told me I would need oars, a cushion, lifejacket, and an anchor. I gathered all my fishing tackle, loaded up, and rowed all the way across the lake; but without one thing—the anchor! You know the slightest wind will cause a boat to drift. A storm moved in quickly and I had no anchor. I was scared to death as I fought the wind. Thankfully, I was able to get back to shore safely.

I think about that fearful day when I go through troubled times in life now. When the storms of life rage against you, did you forget the Anchor? Jesus Christ is our Anchor in a life that gets pretty rough at times. We often turn to other things for comfort when facing a trial. We search for solutions and answers. We must realize it is God that brings peace in the midst of the storm. It is through faith in Him that we know our Anchor holds.

THOUGHTS & REFLECTIONS

_____

_____

_____

_____

_____

_____

_____

THANKSGIVING TURKEY, VENISON & TRADITION

Bless the Lord, O my soul! You who laid the foundations of the earth…He sends the springs into the valleys. They give drink to every beast of the field. By them the birds of the heavens have their home; they sing among the branches. He causes the grass to grow for the cattle. The high hills are for the wild goats. He appointed the moon for seasons; the sun knows its going down. You make darkness…In which all the beasts of the forest creep about…And seek their food from God. O Lord, how manifold are your works!

Selected Verses from Psalm 104 NKJV

When you think of Thanksgiving, you can't help but smell the sweet aroma of a turkey in the oven. I'm sure there are folks around the country that will include some deer tenderloin with their traditional feast. If I were an accomplished cook, I'd give you a venison recipe right now. The operative word in *my* meal preparation is "fried" or "grilled!"

When Thanksgiving morning arrives, my family is gearing up to visit my folks to "knock a tater in the head." In layman's terms: "I'm ready to eat!" One of our long-standing traditions is watching the Detroit Lions play football around noon, and eating at halftime. The rest of the day is spent recovering from gluttony. On Friday, I usually hook up with some buddies and do a little deer hunting at the club.

Having shot a deer prior to Thanksgiving sure takes the pressure off. If you hunt, you know where I'm coming from. It is real easy to become an "evening only" hunter when there is a deer in the freezer. You stay up late the night before a hunt. The alarm sounds off a 4:30 AM, and the temperature outside is in the 20's. I make no move to get up, content with the 9-point buck sitting at the taxidermist. Your buddies are hollering and heckling you, "Come on man, you can sleep anytime…we're at the club to hunt!" Jealousy is a pitiful disease. They can't fathom the thought of you all warm and cozy at the lodge, while they suffer hypothermia with no deer in sight. I understand…misery loves company.

The stories that spawn from these experiences are what life is all about. Thanksgiving is the time of year when deer season is open in most every state. It is an American family tradition. God has blessed us immensely with the opportunity to experience all He so wonderfully created. Most sportsmen would agree He did a fine job, too.

What makes Thanksgiving and hunting such

a strong tradition? It's not football, turkey, or the chance to shoot a big buck. Tradition stems from the hearts of people. It branches out from generation to generation through love and fellowship. A father taking his boy or girl on their first hunt molds tradition. Grandfathers teaching their grandchildren about life through their experiences shape it. Spending time with those you love in the great outdoors solidifies tradition. That, my friends, is a recipe for tradition. May we take the responsibility to carry it on.

THOUGHTS & REFLECTIONS

_____

_____

_____

_____

_____

_____

_____

TIME TO REMEMBER

*O Lord, our Lord, how excellent is Your name in all
the earth…When I consider Your heavens, the work of
Your fingers, the moon and the stars, which You have ordained,
What is man that You are mindful of him…You have made
him to have dominion over the works of Your hands;
You have put all things under his feet…O Lord, our Lord,
How excellent is Your name in all the earth!*
Psalm 8:1, 3, 4, 6, 9 NKJV

For a sportsman, the opening day of deer season should be designated as a National Holiday. We have them for everything else, why not deer season? September 7th is opening day for Bow Season in my home state of North Carolina. Deer hunters get fired up for the big day as if it were the Super Bowl. It's "go" time!

As I sat in my tree stand on opening day of 2002, my heart was filled with emotion as I looked ahead to the first anniversary of perhaps the darkest day in the history of the United States…September 11th, 2001. Many of us can remember where we were when the terrorist attacks were made on that dreadful morning. I had a minute earlier gotten out of the dentist's chair when the dental hygienist said, "I just heard that an airplane crashed into the World Trade Center in New York!" Confused, not yet understanding the crash was premeditated and intentional, I drove down the road toward home. My wife called to inform me a second airplane crashed into the other tower!

As a nation, we have grieved from that moment in time for the citizens, officers, and firemen we lost in those attacks. It is true we had to pick ourselves up and move on. We have done that. However, we must never forget that fateful day and the lives lost and changed forever. Fathers and mothers lost their sons and daughters. Children look for parents who will never come home. How I wish it had all been just a bad dream.

Spending time in the outdoors gives one time to meditate and reflect. Life happens when we least expect it. As you sit and watch all God has created, consider what is truly important and meaningful in life. Take the time to remember.

THOUGHTS & REFLECTIONS

_____

_____

_____

_____

_____

_____

_____

_____

_____

_____

_____

_____

_____

_____

_____

_____

_____

_____

_____

TALK TO THE ANIMALS

Let everything that has breath praise the Lord.
Praise the Lord!

Psalm 150:6 NKJV

We have been amused in years past by animals who "talk" on TV, like "Mr. Ed" or the "singing frog" on cartoons. We've even joked about what we would find out if animals actually could talk. Be honest—we would be in trouble if our pets came clean and spilled the beans.

Have you ever been deer hunting and wondered what a big buck is thinking as he watches you pass by, unaware of his presence? I know it's crazy, but I sure have! In fact, studies have been conducted to see how deer react to hunting pressure. With tracking devices on both the hunter and the hunted, the responses of the deer are recorded as a hunter walks through dense cover. In many instances, the hunter would only be 20 yards from the deer and never know it! This proves my belief that more deer watch us than we ever physically see.

I can just hear a whitetail buck tell his buddy,

"Don't look now, but here comes that guy with the goofy hat!" His buck buddy replies, "He looks a little like Elmer Fudd…hope he has fun freezin' his rear end off again this year!" You know that's what those bucks are thinking. Deer outsmart hunters too often not to have a laugh at our expense.

Have you ever thought about what animals could teach about history if they could talk? Oh, the monumental events they have seen unfold throughout history! Think about the donkey, chickens, and a few sheep in a barn in the one-horse town of Bethlehem. What would they have said about that silent night a young couple rolled into town, only to give birth to a baby they laid in their food trough? I don't believe the wisemen and shepherds were the only ones there to worship baby Jesus.

Read Psalm 150:6 again. Let's remember God's gifts to us as we spend time outdoors. I don't doubt the animals always do.

THOUGHTS & REFLECTIONS

_____

_____

_____

TALK TO THE ANIMALS

_____

_____

_____

_____

_____

_____

_____

_____

_____

_____

_____

_____

_____

_____

_____

_____

_____

_____

_____

DEER STAND DEVOTIONS

Then He said, "Go out, and stand on the mountain before the Lord." And behold, the Lord passed by, and a great and strong wind tore into the mountains and broke the rocks in pieces before the Lord, but the Lord was not in the wind; and after the wind an earthquake, but the Lord was not in the earthquake; and after the earthquake a fire, but the Lord was not in the fire; and after the fire a still small voice.
1 Kings 19:11, 12 NKJV

It is so difficult for us to hear God speaking to our hearts. I believe we are just too busy to listen. Everyone has his or her own daily routine. We work, eat, and sleep most of the time in a 24-hour day. Time management becomes our focus. Where did all the time go? The last I checked, there is the same number of hours in a day now as there was in 1940.

It wasn't too long ago that God, family, and the front porch swings were a way of life for most. There is so much available now to keep us busy and entertained. We panic if we lose the remote control to the TV! Our response is always; "I don't have time!" I am reminded of that the moment I climb up in a deer stand. It is as if God says, "It's about time you slowed down enough so I could talk to you."

What a great opportunity to spend intimate time with our Savior and Lord.

I do pray on the way from the truck to my stand that something doesn't get me in the dark. You know what I'm talking about. It's an hour before daybreak. You're walking up a hollow of dense hardwoods and a bobcat cries out nearby. You wet your pants and start praying, "Lord, just get me up in that deer stand!" We've all been there. It's part of the excitement and thrill of the hunt.

As the sun slowly breaks the tree line, it is as if God turns on a light switch. The once quiet forest comes alive. Birds begin singing, squirrels scratch around, and a mosquito is buzzing in your ear. The beauty and serenity of the moment humbles me. God is never more real to me than at that time.

Regardless of the outcome of the hunt, spend some time with the Lord in prayer. Tell Him what's on your heart and mind. Whatever you might be doing in the outdoors, use the time to draw close to God. Listen with your heart. He is speaking in a still voice.

THOUGHTS & REFLECTIONS

_____

_____

_____

_____

_____

_____

_____

_____

_____

_____

_____

_____

_____

_____

_____

_____

_____

_____

SAFARI JOURNAL

One of the best ways to remember an experience in the outdoors is to put it into words. Yes, a picture can be worth a thousand words, but a mere picture doesn't tell the intimate details of the experience. A picture leaves you to wonder and imagine the adventure. Words, however, give you the "eye-witness" account of the events that took place. Below you will find some of my personal journal entries while on safari in South Africa.

June 4, 2003 – Excited and anxious as we take off from Atlanta. I miss Angie and the boys nonetheless. I thank God for my good friends Pat and Chip. I look forward to the fellowship with them as much as the hunt itself. The flight to Johannesburg will be about 18 hours. I look forward to getting close to the Lord and letting Him teach me more about life through the experience.

June 6, 2003 – I awoke at 6:00 a.m. to the sounds of trickling water and chirping birds. A creek flows below the deck of a picturesque cabana with a grass roof and stonewalls. I feel like I'm Ernest Hemingway or Dr. Livingston on a mission trip. I've got candlelight and the whole nine yards. There are animal tracks right around my hut. I am ready to go eat breakfast before the day's hunt. (Later) We saw an abundance of animals today. Chip harvested a Kudu and Blue Wildebeest. I harvested a Blue Wildebeest and Blesbok.

June 7, 2003 – The country is beautiful. It is so pure and natural—a sportsman's dream! The area is known as the "thorn veldt" because of the many thorn bushes. They provide excellent cover for the game. The topography is rolling hills and ravines, surrounded by mountainous ridges. There are also fields of prairie grass scattered all over. The temperature is about 32 degrees Fahrenheit at night and around 60-65 degrees by day. It is refreshing and invigorating to be outside. Today we walked 10-15 miles. I feel great! Chip and I both harvested Zebra stallions. Pat shot a nice Kudu bull. The new animals we saw include Mountain Reedbuck, Waterbuck,

Nyala, and a Spitting Cobra. The Cobra was in the road. He rose up and flared out his hood at me! Awesome!

June 8, 2003 – At 35 yards, I saw a Giraffe that must have been 18 feet tall if it was a foot. I also saw Impala, Grey Duiker, and Warthog. I harvested a nice Impala. I have gotten to know the staff much better and have developed somewhat of a relationship with them. They are sweet people. I have seen some of the most beautiful sunrises and sunsets ever. The red sky over the Drakensburg Mountains as the sun sets is breathtaking. My friend Pat is a tall, heavyset fellow. The Zulus call him "Mafuta," meaning "fat" or "big." We were told that the Zulu people believe being large and fat is a sign of wealth. When informed of their belief, Pat said, "If that's the case, then they must think I'm a millionaire!"

June 10, 2003 – I've had diarrhea since last night. I woke up from a nap today and was sick with nausea, chills, and weak—the works. I've been doctored by the staff and feel a little better. I couldn't eat supper tonight. Maybe a good night's sleep will help.

June 11, 2003 – So much for the good nights sleep! I didn't sleep a wink until 6:00 a.m.—vomiting and diarrhea all night. Don't know if it's something I ate or a virus. I'm dehydrated from the hard hunting and loss of fluids. Being sick as a dog is a humbling experience, especially on another continent and away from home. Despite the fun I've had, the sickness makes you realize what is truly important— God, Angie, and the boys…home. I just wanted to be home with those that love and care for me. Out here in the bush you feel so alone and helpless. It has been a real "wilderness" experience the last day and night. Could Jesus have felt this way when He spent 40 days in the wilderness? Hungry…helpless… tempted by the devil himself? Maybe this is a test of faith? Hope that God will sustain me. I need you O' Lord. As Psalm 42:1 says, As a deer pants for streams of water, so my soul pants for you O God. Heal my infirmity. Give me rest and bring me home safely to my family.

June 12, 2003 – I must have had a 24-hour stomach virus because I feel much better today. I was able to hunt and harvested a trophy Grey Duiker and another Impala. We have one day left on our trip. It has been a wonderful experience! Nevertheless, Judy Garland was right in the Wizard of Oz when she said, "There's no place like home!"

Take the time to record your hunting or fishing adventure in a diary of journal. If you write it down, your memories will last a lifetime!

THOUGHTS & REFLECTIONS

_____

_____

_____

_____

_____

_____

_____

_____

_____

_____

_____

THE TROPHY KUDU

The earth is the Lord's, and all its fullness,
The world and those who dwell therein.
Psalm 24:1 NKJV

The Kudu that inhabit many parts of Africa are considered the greatest trophy of all the Plain's game animals. A trophy Kudu bull was certainly at the top of my list on my hunt. A mature Kudu bull weighs about 750 lbs on the hoof. Their huge, spiraling horns grow up to 5 feet in length. Like the Rocky Mountain Elk, the Kudu is a majestic and magnificent creation.

Our hunt for a Kudu bull was an adventure and challenge. We started up a mountain at 7:30 a.m. to spot Kudu on the sunny slopes and in the valleys below. Around 8:15 a.m., we spotted two nice bulls in the valley. One of them might have measured 60 inches. My professional hunter Tobie and I moved down the ridge to get closer than 400 yards. The big bull spotted us on the slope and the two of them headed out of the valley and up another ridge. We tracked them to the top of that ridge. The big bull was gone but the other moved into the valley on the other side. At 300 yards, I rested my 7 mm mag. in the fork of a tree and fired a shot. It found its mark.

The bull didn't go down with that first shot, so we closed in. I took 7 more shots at different points in the valley before he was down for good. The Kudu's spiral horns had a 2 ½ turn and measured 52 inches. The beast weighed over 700 lbs. The hunt was a success after a 4-hour stalk. I was worn out, but the supreme challenge made the hunt memorable and gratifying. I thanked God upon reaching the downed animal. I have the utmost respect and admiration for any animal harvested. Whether the quarry is Gray Squirrel or African Kudu, may we never take God's Creation for granted.

THOUGHTS & REFLECTIONS

The Trophy Kudu

WARTHOG IN CAMP

> *But the Lord said to Samuel,*
> *"Do not look at his appearance or at his physical stature…*
> *For the Lord does not see as man sees;*
> *for man looks at the outward appearance,*
> *but the Lord looks at the heart."*
> 1 Samuel 16:7 NKJV

The sun rose slowly on the South African horizon. The Kudu and Impala emerged from the bush to sun themselves after a cold night in June. Herds of Blue Wildebeest and Zebra were not far behind as the "dark continent" gave way to light. We were ready to experience the thrill of the hunt.

After miles of stalking the elusive Plain's game animals that morning, my friend Chip and I headed back to the Umsuluzi Riverside Lodge for brunch. The Zulu staff had set up a beautiful display of meat and fruit in a picnic area on the bank of the river. Our mouths watering, we walked down a set of stone steps to this oasis on the river.

With all the food on the table, a sweet, young Zulu girl took our order for bacon, eggs, and hash browns. No grits, but I felt closer to North Carolina with the "Southern Africa" breakfast. Engaged in conversation, Chip suddenly got quiet and looked with shock over my shoulder toward the steps. I turned my head to see a Warthog starring at us from the top step!

The monstrous Warthog had 7-inch tusks protruding from its bottom jaw. With a reddish-gray mane and tail, this thing was the devil incarnate. Without hesitation, the beast walked down the steps toward us. We jumped up and stood behind the table for protection. The Warthog bumped its snout up under the table in an effort to turn it over. I soon realized the animal was in search of food other than us. "What are we going to do?"

I asked. Chip answered, "I'm going to get my gun from the truck and shoot it!" I told him to let me try and scare it off by banging two chairs together.

My plan was worked. The Warthog reluctantly moved back up the steps. Just as it reached the top of the stairs, Chip fired a shot from my right. The Warthog folded like a cheap lawn chair only 10 feet from me! Alarmed by the shot, the entire camp staff ran to the edge of the deck and looked wide-eyed at the fallen animal. One of them exclaimed, "You've shot the camp pet!" My heart sank. Upon further inspection, the Warthog had a small tag in its ear with its name on it! I could only think of Pumba, the lovable Warthog in the movie The Lion King. We had been at the lodge several days and no one had mentioned a pet Warthog. Chip was only trying to protect us from what looked to be a dangerous wild animal. Honest mistake.

When I ordered bacon and eggs that morning, I didn't expect to have to butcher the hog myself. The poor Warthog was harmless—but it sure didn't look like it! Aren't you glad God doesn't pass judgment on us based on our appearance or superficiality? The Bible says in 1 Samuel 16:7 (NKJV), Man looks on the outward appearance, but the Lord looks at the heart. No matter what people say or think about you, God looks below the surface. He always loves us…"warts" and all!

THOUGHTS & REFLECTIONS

_____

_____

_____

_____

LIVING IN A SHELL

While flounder fishing in a tidewater creek in South Carolina, I noticed an abundance of hermit crabs in the shallow water. I was busy laying out the flounder by jigging a white split-tail grub, equipped with a light-action spinning rod and 6-lb. test line. The flounder were in 4 ft. of water feeding on minnows as the tide fell early in the morning.

I had already caught and released three fish over 14 inches when I hooked the granddaddy in the flounder family. The fish led me up and down the creek. He looked to be about 2 ft. long as it pulled line from my reel. A flounder will turn that body sideways and give you a real fight. It would have been the biggest flounder I'd ever caught. The key words being "would have been," as the fish broke my line. Defeated, I walked to the bank.

Again, I noticed those hermit crabs crawling

all over the sandy bottom. I decided I would take a couple with me to show to my one-year old son. Every time you pick up a shell, the crab retreats out of sight. Hidden deep within his shell, the hermit crab is safe from predators. I couldn't help but feel sorry for the little fellows. They have to lug that shell with them wherever they go.

How much are we like the hermit crab? We too spend much of our lives in a shell. We feel vulnerable and at risk in many areas of our lives. So we would rather withdraw into our shell than risk being hurt or wounded. Living life in a shell, we're unable to experience all God has for us. We do the same in relationships with others. As soon as we feel threatened, we pull back and hide.

We all have a shell of some kind. Sure they can be protective, even beautiful on the outside. But they can also be heavy and cumbersome. We haul that thing around as a defense mechanism. We can receive so much from God and others if we just lose the shell! Jesus Christ bore our sin and shame on the cross so that we wouldn't have to carry that old shell around anymore. We are free!

THOUGHTS & REFLECTIONS

_____

_____

_____

_____

_____

_____

_____

_____

_____

_____

_____

_____

_____

_____

_____

_____

_____

_____

_____

SOAR LIKE AN EAGLE

But those who hope in the LORD will renew their strength.
They will soar on wings like eagles; they will run and
not grow weary, they will walk and not be faint.
Isaiah 40:31 NIV

The American Bald Eagle symbolizes the freedom of the United States. This majestic bird represents life, liberty, and the pursuit of something better. I have seen only two Bald Eagles in the wild. The first was on the way to a deer hunt one afternoon. I saw an eagle soaring high above a mountain peak. I almost wrecked my truck as I gazed in amazement. Thank you, Lord, for such an awesome sight!

The second sighting took place in Michigan. I was perch fishing when I saw a Bald Eagle gracefully fly across the water with a fish in its talons. It landed in the top of a tree to enjoy his catch. I almost fell out of my boat as I witnessed the event. I think the eagle caught more fish than I did that day.

These experiences made me think of Isaiah 40:31. You can understand why Isaiah chose the eagle to make that point. An eagle soars higher than all other species of bird. While other fowl live close to the ground, the eagle flies high atop the food chain. His view is better than any bird. God is telling us in His Word to soar like an eagle. As His children, we are to live high above the world's standards. We are not here to lead mediocre lives; rather, we can fly high like the eagle.

THOUGHTS & REFLECTIONS

_____

_____

_____

_____

_____

_____

_____

_____

_____

_____

_____

LOST AT SEA

"He who enters by the door is the shepherd of the sheep. To him the doorkeeper opens, and the sheep hear his voice; and he calls his own sheep by name and leads them out. And when he brings out his own sheep, he goes before them; and the sheep follow him, for they know his voice. Yet they will by no means follow a stranger, but will flee from him, for they do not know the voice of strangers" I am the good shepherd; and I know My sheep, and am known by My own.
John 10:2-5, 14 NKJV

All right, it really wasn't a "sea" I was lost on a year ago. It sure makes for a good title, though. Actually, I was on Fontana Lake in the North Carolina Mountains. The lake is quite remote, absent of any residential or commercial development. You can just about get lost on that lake in broad daylight, let alone at night.

Some friends and I were small-mouth bass fishing on a warm spring evening. We had caught several nice fish when a dense fog set in on the lake. I'd never seen anything like it in all my days! You literally couldn't see your hand in front of your face! We had our running lights on and hollered for help, but to no avail. We had to drop anchor to keep from drifting into the bank. My friend's father was in another boat further down the lake. It was hours until we heard a faint voice calling, "Boys, where are you?" My buddy immediately recognized his father. "Daddy!" he yelled back. Soon after, we were all found and made it safely home.

Did you know that a flock of sheep recognizes only the voice of their shepherd? Our Scripture points out this interesting truth. Jesus Christ is our Shepherd; and we are His sheep. He calls us with a still, small voice only we can hear. He seeks to love and tend to us. When we are lost, He leads us home. Respond to the Lord when He calls you by name. You'll know His voice.

THOUGHTS & REFLECTIONS

_____

_____

_____

_____

MAN'S BEST FRIEND

God demonstrates His own love toward us,
in that while we were still sinners, Christ died for us.
Romans 5:8 NKJV

Dogs have long been referred to as "man's best friend." How many of us had a dog as a childhood pet? I'm not talking about cats now, just "good ol' dawgs!" I got my first dog at the age of 10. He was the pick of the litter, a mixed breed of Golden Lab and Brittany spaniel. His name was Rusty.

Rusty was everything to everybody...a friend, guardian, and a pretty good bird-dog too. We put up many a covey of quail together. Back at the house, he would tree a squirrel or raccoon in a minute. Rusty and I shared some special times together. Through my laughter and my tears, he was always there, as warm and faithful as the sunrise in the morning. Rusty passed away at the age of 14. I couldn't help but cry and grieve over the loss of such a wonderful companion. Thank you Lord for such a blessing.

You know God, too, wants to be "man's best friend." He loves us unconditionally and waits for us when we stray away. I'll never forget Rusty anxiously looking out the window as the car rolled into the drive. God's love for us is even greater than a faithful "ol' dawg" while He waits for us to come home to Him. Thank you Lord for such an even greater blessing.

THOUGHTS & REFLECTIONS

_____

_____

_____

_____

_____

_____

_____

_____

_____

_____

NO PLACE LIKE HOME

> *Jesus said to him, "You shall love the Lord your God with all your heart, with all your soul, and with all your mind. This is the first and great commandment."*
> Matthew 22:38, 38 NKJV

It is a fact that the vast majority of hunters are men. With that said, listen up men!

As the North Carolina deer season drew to a close, I grew anxious to hunt just a few more times. I managed to sneak off on a Saturday morning to my honey hole on a private farm close to home. The temperature was freezing and rainy. It wasn't long before I was ready to head for the house. The deer probably watched me shiver in the stand and thought, "This guy is either dedicated or stupid!" A little of both I reckon. Maybe I deserved a little punishment for not staying home that morning. My wife and boy wanted me to stay, with things to do and fun to have. I hunted anyway and didn't see a cotton pickin' thing. Not even a squirrel, let alone a deer. God humbles us to show us what our priorities are and what they should be.

The great Vince Lombardi once said that his loyalty was to "God, family, and the Green Bay Packers." Where do we put our hobbies and interests in our list of priorities? I am as passionate as anyone when it comes to the outdoors, but fail to show such passion consistently for the Lord and my loved ones. Sometimes it takes a cold, miserable experience to help us realize that there is no place like home. Thank you God for showing us what is truly important in life. Our relationships with God and family are far more important than hanging an 8-pointer on the wall. I guess I'll just have to ask my wife to go hunting with me next time. Just kidding Lord!

Thoughts & Reflections

_____

_____

_____

_____

_____

_____

IN HIS SIGHTS

Are not two sparrow sold for a copper coin?
And not one of them falls to the ground apart from
your Father's will. But the very hairs of your head are
all numbered. Do not fear therefore;
you are of more value than many sparrows.
Matthew 10:29-31 NKJV

Hunting equipment has come a long way with technological advancements made over the last several years. There seems to be a gadget that serves any purpose you can think of—from bow quivers to gun scopes.

The new in-line muzzleloaders have an effective range that is comparable to many rifles. I'm still using the old 50 caliber hammerlock if you're wondering. Missed a deer this past season with it too! The quality of hunting optics and scopes on the market is unbelievable. You can buy a riflescope now that gathers so much light, you can practically hunt at night if it were legal. (I hope you're not one of those that do anyway!) We have long referred to putting a scope on an animal as having the animal "in your sights." Think about the times you've seen a buck come into view. You ease your rifle up, look through the scope or open sights, steady the crosshairs on the buck, and say to yourself, "I've got him in my sights…boom!"

You know, God hunts for man in the same way. He is intently scanning the world in His search for you and I to have a personal relationship with Him. Jesus Christ even called his disciples to be "fishers of men." It is important to remember that as God looks for us and calls us by name, we need to respond to Him in faith. Through some of the most troubled times of my life, I know that God kept a watchful eye on me. Do you know God personally and intimately? If so, you have the blessed assurance that you will always be "in His sights."

Thoughts & Reflections

_____

_____

_____

_____

THE ONE THAT GOT AWAY

*O Jerusalem, Jerusalem…How often I wanted to gather
your children together, as a hen gathers her chicks under
her wings, but you were not willing!*
Matthew 23:37 NKJV

Anglers have forever told their stories about "the one that got away," or in my case, the "many" that got away. I am haunted to this day by the memory of a brook trout that got away in a small stream in the mountains of North Carolina.

One of my favorite honey holes was Upper Bowlens Creek near Mount Mitchell. At the time, this small creek offered some of the best brook trout fishing in the state. Fly-fishing with a Tellico nymph, I caught and released about 20 fish as I worked my way downstream. Brook trout, commonly referred to as "specks" by locals, don't grow much larger than the length of your hand. As a rule of thumb in those parts, a speck over 12 inches is a true wall hanger. As I approached the largest hole in that stretch of water, I let the current carry my nymph along a steep bank and under a large boulder. I quickly noticed that the fly had come to an abrupt halt so I gave a little jerk as I thought I was hung up. As I pulled firmly to free up the nymph, out rolled the biggest, most beautiful, blood-red brook trout you have ever seen. With God as my witness, the fish was a foot long if it was an inch! As a matter of fact, it already had a wood plaque attached to it and a brass plate engraved with my name and the date (Okay, not so fast Tom). Before I could land the trophy, it threw that fly right back in my face. Prozac anyone? Depression set in real quick as I headed straight for the truck. Do not pass go. Do not collect $200! Do not mount a trophy today!

Did you know that God in Heaven grieves over people who are lost and wandering without purpose? He "fishes for men" through His Son, Jesus, and doesn't like to go home skunked. His desire is to have a personal relationship with you and me. If you've never experienced it, simply ask Jesus Christ to come into your heart and life as your Savior and Lord. May God never have to refer to you as "the one that got away."

THOUGHTS & REFLECTIONS

_____

_____

_____

_____

_____

_____

_____

_____

_____

_____

_____

_____

_____

_____

_____

_____

_____

_____

MAJOR IN MEN, MINOR IN FISH

And Jesus, walking by the Sea of Galilee, saw two brothers, Simon called Peter, and Andrew his brother, casting a net into the sea; for they were fishermen. Then He said to them, "Follow Me, and I will make you fishers of men." They immediately left their nets and followed Him.

Matthew 4:18-20 NKJV

It's no surprise why Jesus used parables and stories to make a point. He spoke in terms that were relevant to the people around Him. Many of His parables had something to do with the outdoors, including fishing, farming or building. Why? Because that's what most of the folks could relate to, just as we do today.

Read Matthew 4:18-20 once again. Jesus met Simon Peter and Andrew while they were fishing. The brothers were probably members of the Galilee Chapter of Bass Masters. They fished for a living; maybe they were even on the Galilee tournament trail! Here comes a stranger, Jesus, who says, "Come follow me, and I will make you fishers of men." How they responded to His call made all the difference in their lives. They didn't say, "Let us think about it a few days" or "Let me talk it over with my wife and

I'll get back to ya." In absolute faith, the Bible says they immediately stopped what they were doing and followed Him.

Now I have fished all my life and I don't plan on quitting anytime soon. But are we as diligent in sharing our faith with others as we are catching fish? It doesn't necessarily mean you have to sell your tackle and boat (unless you value your bass boat more than your wife!) God wants us to focus on eternal things. A friend coming to know Christ personally and going to heaven is a whole lot more important than the 10-lb. largemouth bass you want to hang on the wall. Think about switching your major to "men," and your minor to "fish."

THOUGHTS & REFLECTIONS

_____

_____

_____

_____

_____

THE GREAT KENTUCKY FLOOD

The grass withers, the flower fades, but the word of our God stands forever.
Isaiah 40:8 NKJV

In the mountains of Southeastern Kentucky, there lies the sleepy little town of Pineville. Pineville, the county seat for Bell County, was the home place of my mother's family. We often took family trips to there to visit my great-grandparents, Mamaw and Papaw Black.

They loved to fish together in the TVA rivers and lakes that made up the region. As a young boy, I could see Jesus Christ glorified through their lives. They were simple folks with a simple faith, lacking nothing in terms of necessity. Mamaw is the reason to this day that when asked what my favorite food is, I proudly exclaim, "Biscuits and gravy!" She made the best milk gravy known to man in that ol' black skillet. Her southern-fried chicken wasn't too bad either.

In the 1970's, a massive flood hit Pineville and practically destroyed the whole town. It was surrounded on all sides by ridges, while the river passed through it. With days of torrential rainfall, the floodwaters engulfed the entire town. Once the water receded, Mamaw and Papaw returned home to survey the damage. Mud and silt had destroyed everything in sight. Upon further investigation, they noticed the family Bible sitting on the coffee table in its usual place. I can remember seeing that Bible there my whole life. The Bible was unharmed by the flood! There wasn't a watermark on a single page! It sounds unbelievable, but is the absolute truth. God had protected the one thing that was most precious to them.

Mamaw and Papaw knew the power of the Word. While they lost furniture, clothes, and memorable pictures, their Bible was kept safe from the flooding water. No matter what storms of life you face, God's Word will always remain the same. Its power and presence in our lives will forever be unchanged.

THOUGHTS & REFLECTIONS

TRAIL OF TEARS

Let your light so shine before men, that they may see your good works and glorify your Father in Heaven.
Matthew 5:16 NKJV

Native Americans hold a special place in the history of the United States. We can talk about "God's Country," but nobody appreciated it more than those who came before us. They were quite the outdoorsmen—proficient in hunting, trapping, and fishing. Imagine a time when God's Creation was unspoiled by modern civilization.

From my mother's side of the family in the mountains of Southeastern Kentucky, I am proud to carry Cherokee blood. My Mamaw Black often bragged on my jet-black hair, a trait inherited from past generations. "As black as coal," she would claim. It has long been a living reminder of the Cherokee history of tradition and tragedy. The Cherokee people were forced to move from their native land in a march of what became known as the "Trail of Tears."

I had the privilege of working closely with the

Cherokee as an insurance agent in the early 90's. It was my first job out of college. The agency served the Eastern Band of the Cherokee Indians in the Great Smokey Mountains of North Carolina. If you were to look in the file cabinet at the office, you would find many last names derived from the outdoors: Running Deer, Standing Deer, Climbing Bear, Owl, Crow, Feather, Rattler, Cucumber, and the list goes on. "Yes Mr. Climbing Bear, your policy will be effective tomorrow" was a common occurrence! Every once in a while, one of the elder Cherokee would come to the office and couldn't speak a word of English. I'll never forget the burley fellow from the Owl family that paid his insurance premiums with money he made by hunting ginseng.

What can we learn from our Native American ancestors? Just as they were persecuted years ago, Christians have long suffered in the same way. In a sinful world, it is not always popular to take a stand for Christ. In the midst of darkness, we are called to "let our light shine before men." Government legislation and intervention stifles the values and principals this country was founded on.

No one understands better what the Cherokee Indians endured than Jesus Christ. Take the time to read Luke 23:26-43. After being beaten and scorned, He carried his cross to another place, a hill called Golgotha. The road that led to Calvary was a "trail of tears" for our Savior and Lord. However, it was in that painful journey and experience that we find forgiveness, hope, and eternal life.

THOUGHTS & REFLECTIONS

_____

_____

_____

_____

_____

_____

_____

_____

_____

_____

ROLES & RESPONSIBILITIES

*So the sky, the earth, and all that filled them were finished…
And there was no person to care for the ground…
Then the LORD God took dust from the ground and formed
a man from it. He breathed the breath of life into
the man's nose, and the man became a living person.
Then the LORD God planted a garden…called Eden, and
put the man He had formed into it…to care for it and to work it.*
Genesis 2:1, 5, 7, 8, 15 NCV

It is a fact that God created the heavens and the earth. Were there outdoorsmen back in Bible times? Are you kidding? Deer hunters were heading for the woods long before Jesus was born.

As outdoorsmen of the present, we have been ordained with the responsibility of conserving our wildlife and their habitats. Who better to answer the call than we who appreciate and enjoy His Creation. How can we help? The purchase of licenses is one way. In addition, help may be given through financial support or volunteer work with any number of wildlife and environmental organizations. It is always a good rule to leave the land in better shape than when you arrived. Pick up trash, plant food plots, maintain wildlife habitat, and so on.

"Father God, thank you for the wonderful gift of Creation you have entrusted to us. May we boldly accept this awesome responsibility and take an active role in preservation and conservation of the land you have given us."

THOUGHTS & REFLECTIONS

_____

_____

_____

_____

_____

_____

_____

_____

_____

_____

_____

_____

_____

_____

_____

_____

_____

_____

_____

_____

_____

_____

_____

_____

_____

_____

_____

_____

_____

_____

_____

VENISON PEPPER STEAK & RICE

2 lb. venison round steak
1/2 cup flour
1/2 teaspoon salt
1/2 teaspoon pepper
1 large onion, sliced
6 oz. mushrooms, sliced
4 teaspoons Worcestershire sauce
1 large green pepper, remove seeds, slice
1 cup water, cooking oil, minute white rice

Cut steaks into 1" strips 3" long. Coat strips with mix of flour, salt and pepper. Heat oil over medium heat in large fry pan and lightly brown meat. Drain excess oil. Add onion, mushrooms, green pepper and Worcestershire sauce. Stir fry for 10 minutes. Add water, cover and simmer for 30 minutes. While the pepper steak is simmering, put some minute rice in boiling water. Serve pepper steak over white rice. Enjoy.

Serves: 4

BIOGRAPHY

Thomas E. Naumann lives with his wife and two sons in Union County, North Carolina. He came to a saving knowledge of Jesus Christ as a young boy. He graduated as a Grayson Scholar from Mars Hill College in the mountains of western NC. He is the President/Founder of Cherokee Run Hunting Lodge LLC and EATSLEEPHUNT.com, a hunting lodge and website, that seek to glorify God through His Creation, and call outdoorsmen to a greater responsibility to respect and conserve all wildlife and their habitats. Around the Campfire was inspired by his passion for the Lord and the outdoors.

ACKNOWLEDGMENTS

I would like to thank a few folks for their support and encouragement in helping make this book a reality.

To my best friend and wife Angie, for her unwavering love and encouragement from the beginning.

To my blessed boys Tucker and Tanner, you make life so much fun. You are truly God's opinion that life should go on.

To my huntin' buddies David Beaver, Chip Ferguson, Robby Williams, Mike Leopard, Ed Horstkamp and Pat Kelly for their friendship and prayerful support.

To my mother-in-law Linda Embrey, for her strong faith and tender heart.

To my brother-in-law and sister, Randy and Chrisy Hatcher, for believing in the vision and me.

To my younger brother Tim, for teaching me the true meaning of dedication and commitment.

To my dear mother Bev Naumann, for introducing me to Jesus Christ at a young age. Her unconditional love for God, family, and others is beyond compare.

To my father Jim Naumann, for always being there for me in the good times and the bad.

To my Lord and Savior, Jesus Christ for saving me by His grace. When the storms of life blow, He is my shelter and strength.

To the many others in my life who have made a difference in me along the way.